Inspired Words

Dear John & Alex
 So much fun
to be with you!

♡ Mimi

Sculptures
Paintings
Inspired Words

Anne Mimi Sammis

Foreword by
Ruth Shilling

All One World Books & Media

Copyright © 2019 by Anne Mimi Sammis

All rights reserved.

Cover painting and all artwork within this book:
Anne Mimi Sammis

Cover and book design: Ruth Shilling

Published by:
All One World Books & Media
www.all1world.com
PO Box 422, West Kingston, RI 02892
USA

ISBN: 978-1-945963-55-1

"Anne Mimi Sammis' sculpture
embraces a form of
peace,
the inherent goodness and readiness of
love and acceptance in humankind.

Mimi's art makes us all wish for
a continuation of the UN's mission of
peace
in every nook and cranny of this world."

Agnes Gund, President
The Museum of Modern Art, New York

"Mimi Sammis' work celebrates the miracle of life
and the great age-old concepts of
love, peace, forgiveness, hope, and vision
which helps humanity on
its mysterious journey in the universe."

Dr. Robert Muller
Chancellor of the United Nations'
University of Peace

"Thinly painted clouds, sky and yellow-green fields,
her canvasses maintain an austerity and
mood of gentle realization of nature's
tough, intense beauty."

Art World

"The creative energy that
Mimi finds in this process of bronze casting
is reflected in her exuberant,
yet graceful figurative sculptures.
Whether they are dancing with abandon
or reaching for the heavens,
Sammis' human forms
express a freedom of movement that becomes
a metaphor for the artist's convictions."

Nancy Whipple Grinnell, Curator
Newport Art Museum, Newport, RI

Dedication

There have been so many people
who have walked this walk with me.
I'd like to give my heartfelt gratitude to each
and every one of them.

Without my late husband Pat,
my father,
my children and family,
none of this would have happened.

Ruth's friendship and total dedication to this
project cannot be measured in words.

I love you all!

Mimi ♥

Contents

List of Artworks	x
Foreword by Ruth Shilling	xi
Preface by Mimi	xiii
Sculptures, Paintings, Inspired Words	1
More About Mimi	69
Additional Book Suggestions	76

List of Artworks

Front Cover: Woman with Dove
Back Cover: Dance of Peace
i   Dancing Family of Three
vii   Rebirth
ix   Above: Dancing Family of Five
    Below: Moon on Narragansett Bay
xi   Spiraling
xiii   Above: St. Francis
    Below: Golden Light
xv   Up You Go
1   Tsunami of Love
3   Mother of All
5   Above: Crashing Waves
    Below: Yellow Trees
7   Angel of Peace
9   Above: Poetic Sand Dunes
    Below: Pink Hydrangeas
11   Horse with Three Girls
13   Moon on Breaking Surf
15   Above: Ring Around the Rosie
    Below: Dancing Family of Four
17   Above: Summer Birches
    Below: Winter Birches
19   Above: Heart of the World
    Below: Tree on Hill
21   Above: Moon Over Water
    Below: Refection
23   Above: Belle Isle St. Mare No. 1
    Below: Belle Isle St. Mare No. 2
25   Birth of Love
27   Orange River
29   Above: Embrace of Life
    Below: Pounding Surf
31   Rebirth Couple
33   Winter Brook
35   Above: Adirondack View
    Below: Early Morning Fishermen
37   In His Hands
39   Irises
41   Above: Spring Road
    Below: Autumn Road
43   Love
45   Held In Love
47   Dance of Joy
49   Burst of Love
51   Above: Daisies
    Below: Early Morning
53   Enlightenment
55   Father and Son
57   I Am One
59   Above: House in Spain
    Below: Bahama Reflections
61   Walking Together
63   Painting in Blue
65   Above: Rainbow of Souls
    Below: Grandchildren
67   Dove of Peace
75   Dance of Peace

Foreword

by Ruth Shilling

Anne Mimi Sammis, PhD, known as "Mimi" to the many of us who love and admire her, has been an inspiration to people from many walks of life.

Whether it is chatting with whomever she meets while walking on Rhode Island's Narragansett Beach, talking with the Queen of England, or connecting with people from all over the world at the United Nations, Mimi's effervescent presence brings a sparkle to each interaction. A chance meeting with Mimi often makes such an indelible impression that people will remember and recount it vividly years later.

It has been a pleasure and privilege to put together this book with a variety of Mimi's artistic expressions. I am delighted to be able to bring to a wider audience the beauty, joy, and upliftment these pieces exude. I hope this book will fill your heart with its positivity and invitation to see more, enjoy more, and celebrate more!

There are, of course, many more pieces of her art that didn't fit into this small book. We chose ones in a variety of mediums – watercolor, acrylics, pastels, and, of course, the sculptures for which she is most widely known.

The words that are included on the left-hand pages of the book are taken from a November 2018 interview I recorded with Mimi at her home in Rhode Island.

Some of the text relates to the artwork, but most of it should be viewed as separate from the art on the right-hand pages.

To all those who join in the dance of life!

Ruth Shilling
All One World

Note: You can read more about Mimi's many accomplishments in the final section of this book, **More About Mimi** (page 69).

Preface

by Mimi

I have been saying the Saint Francis prayer daily since 1987.

"Lord, make me an instrument of your peace."

It's amazing how this simple prayer has changed my life. I believe this is why I have been used as an instrument of peace and love.

Sculptures

Paintings

Inspired Words

Tsunami of Love

The inspiration of this painting came to me in a dream about a tsunami of LOVE on the earth.
Each day now, I breathe in love, then breathe out love to everyone in the world. Whoosh!

It's been a wonderful way to start my day!

The Mother of All symbolizes
the mother of all creation.

I feel that she is praying for us, and
bringing peace and love and joy to the
world and all those who see her.

She is actually a great big drum.
I had no idea that she was going to be
a drum when I created her.
You can drum on her and send your
prayers out to the world.

It's lots of fun and very powerful.

Mother of All

Beauty

A wonderful thing I have found is
to focus on beauty all day long.

There are so many beautiful things. You can focus on your face in the mirror — this beautiful face that has eyes and ears, everything that works…. You can focus on the beauty in people, their eyes, or the sky or the trees. It's amazing how beautiful everything gets.

I want to see beauty today.
I see beauty everywhere.

Time for joy!

Dance. Be kind. Be nice.

Just show up.
It doesn't have to be perfect.

I learned that trying to be perfect was a way to destroy a painting or a sculpture (by overworking it).

Truth

When I hear truth, it opens my heart,
and who's ever speaking the truth,
I trust in a very different way.

It's so wonderful when someone can speak the truth and you listen in a nonjudgmental way and really wish the best for them. It's like you have their back. They may not even know it, but you are there to support them in a beautiful way. And that's a prayer.

Be still and know that I am God.
Psalm 46:10

Mind and Ego

Your mind does not control you,
unless you let it.
I find it is much better to listen to
my heart or my gut,
rather than my mind.

I have given the ego a job.
I told the ego, "It is very,
very important that you support
my higher self."
Since then, the ego has stopped
nattering at me. It feels it has a very
important job, and it does!

Space Between My Thoughts

We're free when the mind doesn't control us anymore, and we can listen, listen, listen to our intuition.

I used to think that I just thought what I thought. I had no idea that there was

> a space between my thoughts
> and what I <u>wanted</u> to think.

When I learned that, I experienced real power. Meditation was the key for that because I finally was able to still my mind by focusing on my breath.

> Once I did that, I was free.

I can only think one thought at a time,
and
I get to choose what that thought is.

Wish somebody well. That's a prayer.

Don't forget to be happy.
It's so much fun!

Breathe.

I open the door to God's
love and healing.

Forgive myself, love myself.

*If you don't like what you're thinking,
think another thought.
If I don't like what I'm looking at,
I have many other choices of things I can look at, and lots of them are wonderful.*

Thank You

I remember once saying something nice to someone, and they blocked me. They said, "No, no! That's not true!" My heart felt so hurt because I was giving them a gift and they were pushing the gift away. There was no give and take. It created a sadness.

So I realized how important it is, when anyone comes to you and wants to give you anything – a compliment or something kind – to say, "Thank you very much." Keep the energy flow open. Otherwise, you become separated. And that really doesn't feel good.

I am a vessel of peace and love and joy and light.
All I need to do is to sit down,
close my eyes,
visualize light coming into my heart,
and be.

"No unemployed angels!"
They are there waiting to help us,
but we need to ask.

Change

Change is often very difficult because I think I have figured out my life and how things should be. Then suddenly, I am presented with something that I don't want to be different. But if I get quiet and basically surrender, surrender, surrender to God, then change becomes a friend because everything is in divine order.

Handling a Problem

When I am presented with a problem, I try to remember to turn the problem over to the Divine and live in the moment.

So I just say, "I let You have this. Just give me a pleasant moment." Each pleasant moment creates an incredible life.

Anger

I have had a lot of anger in my life. One time I was writing Morning Pages (you write three pages of flow of consciousness), and I decided I was going to write about anger. Well, it was 36 pages later when I finished writing about anger. I had *so* much anger!

> It was buried deep.
> It all came out,
> and I was free.

For me, I think a lot of that anger came from when I felt I was treated unfairly and I buried that anger. I believe you don't bury those feelings dead. You bury them alive, and they live inside you. It's very important to unleash those memories, so they don't dwell in your body and your soul and your mind and control you. There are many ways to release anger in a safe way, and it is well worth doing.

What Do I Want?

If we don't have any thoughts about what we want, then when we get it, we won't even know that it's what we wanted. We won't know to be grateful for it.

A Force That Wants the Very Best for Me

Often things will pop into my head. Reminders like, "You left the pot on the stove," or "Don't forget to call that person. You're supposed to be having lunch with them." I think it's important to know these thoughts are coming from somewhere. Something is reminding me.

There is some force here for my highest good. There's something that has my back. There is some force that wants the very best for me. And that is the force I connect with.

Praying Together

I love praying with people. I'll get an intuition, "This person might benefit from a prayer." So, I'll ask them, "Would you like a prayer?" Usually people say, yes. Someone else might be present, so I'll ask them if they would like to join us.

It's so beautiful when we all pray together. You can feel a real shift in the energy.

After I pray, I like to ask them to pray, too, because it's very powerful when we open up our hearts and ask for help. At the end of the prayer we say,

> "This or something better
> is now manifesting for the highest
> good of all concerned."

Often, we don't know what's for our highest good. We don't know what painful experiences are teaching us sometimes. We don't know why unhappy things happen

to people. When we turn it over and say, "This or something better is now manifesting for the highest good of all concerned," that means the Divine is in charge and we have surrendered.

Prayer is very powerful.

*Have you thought of what
your higher self might want?
It's clear when you
put your hands on your heart
and listen.*

*Personal power for me is God power.
It's letting the ego go and listening
and acting with divine purpose.*

*It was hard for me to grow up.
I had to take responsibility, and
I didn't want to do that.
But then,
once I started to take responsibility,
I really liked it, and it made me free.*

Past Present Future

There is so much we cannot control. Being in my head in the past or the future is not helpful to me, but living in this moment is a wonderful way to live.

The past is over. If I am going to live in the past, it is almost a form of indulgence because I could be using that time to do something wonderful right now. Instead, I am thinking about how I wish it had been or what I want it to be, and that means I am not really living.

You can't create in the past.
You can only create in the moment.

Wish what you wish for the future, and then let go of it and accept what happens.

Choosing My Actions

If I want to have power,
I have a space in between
whatever might be bothering me
and what I might want.

I detach with love and allow some time
to choose what my action will be.

Inspiration

Inspiration, for me, is
seeing something that touches my heart,
and then, if it is something
I want to paint,
to paint it immediately
(or at least take a photograph).

Zip the Lip

I have found that most of the time, anger directed at people doesn't work out. For one thing, you lose your power. They're the ones in control. So I have found I just "zip the lip," and deal with it somehow later to get it out. But to have control, so I don't become a bigger part of the problem. What happens if a war is declared and no one shows up?

If I don't show up for someone's anger, there is a much better chance of the problem getting resolved. That doesn't mean I have to take abuse or unkindness, but it does mean that I give some space in between so that I make a good decision about what to do. And it definitely doesn't mean to bury the anger. Somewhere, I need to bring the anger out and release it — with a friend or writing about it or…. It's a whole process.

My Happiness Is Not Dependent on What They Do; It's What I Do.

Once I got it that I became more powerful by not getting angry (I became the powerful one because I was in control of my emotions), it made it easier not to get angry because I didn't feel like a victim. Once you get in the game of reacting, you become a victim again, because you are afraid — that they are going to hurt you in some way, take something away from you, or not give you what you want....

Once you can detach from reacting, you become very powerful. You grow up and you realize that your happiness is not dependent on what they do; it's what <u>you</u> do. Self-control really enables that. It means sometimes you don't get what you think you want or what you think you need, but you get something much bigger.

Giving and Receiving

I didn't like to ask for help. I felt that if I asked for help, then I would have to give. When I started to give, it felt so good I wanted to give more, and then I was willing to ask for help.

Now there are so many things that I have to ask for help with. There's no way I can make these big sculptures alone. There's no way I can make the little sculptures alone. When I am in the foundry, I look at all these people helping me, and I think, "How did I ever end up here?"

Now, I ask lots of people for help. If anyone comes to my house, I'll ask them to move a chair or move a box or whatever. People are happy to help. So I found that it's about giving and receiving. I feel that if you can receive, then you have more to give.

Growth

It's kind of like a plant. In order to grow, I need to be nurtured by many things. And I need to accept that nurturance — from the sun or the air or the soil. Accepting help has been a huge part of my growth.

Change or Suffer

A lot of growth has happened in my life when I couldn't control or change things. At those times I had to change or suffer.

Love

Love, for me, is opening the heart and not being afraid to express something beautiful, whether or not you say it in words or it's a feeling.

You can send love out through your heart and never even say a word. You can send love out through your eyes by just looking at someone.

Talking to my Higher Power

A lot of people say, "Just surrender everything to God," but I don't believe that because the God of my understanding wants communication with me, and wants to hear what I want, wants to hear my desires.

So I am learning to spend time communicating and talking to my Higher Power about _everything_. Absolutely everything. No secrets, no little hidden nooks and crannies, but just being totally open.

If I am concerned about someone or I want something, I want to discuss that with this force that has the best intention for me. And then I can let go of it.

Goals and Expectations

I believe in having goals but not expectations.

The goals are what I would like to have happen. My major goal is to have happen what the divine plan for me is. But I have never seen anything wrong with making goals, as long as I don't hold onto them and have a lot of expectations that are going to be painful when they don't work out, because really, I do not know what is for my highest good.

That's why I need to let go of the future. It all happens in the moment.

Spreading Love

It's easy to make myself happy. For one thing, when I see people and they say, "How are you?" I say, "I am better for seeing you!" And I mean that. I really am better for seeing them. Little things that we do, like smiling at somebody or saying a kind word, can shift someone's day.

When I leave people, I like to leave them a little better than when I first saw them. It's so easy to think of something beautiful. Even if you say, "Oh, look how beautiful that tree is," or "What a lovely day." Just something nice.

It's made my life so much better because I feel as if I have a mission in life, and my mission is, basically, to spread love.

Prayer

Prayer is easy.
I just sit down, close my eyes, watch my breath, and the mind gets still. Phew!

When in need, the best prayer is,
"Help. Help. Help.
Bring it on. I'm ready!"

Win-Win Intention

I believe in win-win situations — where everyone wins. There is a way to do that. When you set the intention that everyone wins, it will happen.

Walk Away

*I definitely don't believe in having anyone abuse me. You can walk away with your mind or your feet.
We're not kids. We can walk away.*

Sometimes I just listen to people and I don't open my mouth. Often people want to just talk and talk. Well, I let them just keep talking, and then they look me and say, "Did you hear me?" And I say, "Yes. I'm listening." And finally they have talked it all out.

I don't give a response. They get to talk and I get to listen. Then I get to choose what I want to physically do with my life, or mentally do with my life or spiritually with my life. <u>I</u> <u>get</u> <u>to</u> <u>choose</u>.

*That's the thing about growing up.
<u>I</u> am in charge of my emotions.*

Every Aspect of Our Lives

Our divine self wants to be a part of every single aspect of our lives. Not just the big important things, but everything — the way I get up in the morning, the way I walk, the way I eat, my conversations, what happens in my life, what I am looking at... It wants to hear about that. It wants to hear about the people I am concerned about in my life.

So I am learning to trust and turn things over, and I am getting beautiful answers and a great feeling of connection.

Before, I thought I was not important enough to have that kind of connection with any Source. But now I am learning that it is very powerful to do that.

The New Zealanders say, "God has manners. He doesn't come in unless you ask him."

Individuals Serving Together as One

Separation is the cause of all pain. For a child, being separated from his mother is painful. If you got separated from one of your limbs, it would be very painful. Being separated from your God is painful.

So I have learned that we are all one, each playing our part, AND it's fun to interact with each other.

It reminds me of the human body, how every aspect has its own individuality, but they all serve together to make the whole body work.

Inspirations

Sometimes I get inspired in meditation to do a sculpture, and if I don't do it, it slips away. But sometimes, it will be so persistent that it will natter at me.

One time, Spirit wanted me to do a TV show for PBS. Every single day for two years, it told me, "Do the TV show." It wouldn't stop until I did it.

Do It

When I feel inspired, I am learning not to put it off, but to stay with the inspiration and to make it become physical reality — either in an action, a word or a creative work of art.

If I get inspired, DO IT.

Or as my father would say,
"Easy does it, but <u>do</u> <u>it</u>."

Freedom

Freedom is really being myself
and being able to express that in safety,
and sometimes, not even in safety.

Freedom is being able to
be my loving self.

Daily Practices

For me, the value of doing a daily practice is that it is a life changer. It might be to meditate, to stretch, to walk, or even to find something to laugh about every day. Doing something consistently has more power than doing it sporadically because once it starts to be sporadic, the next step is to stop doing it all together. If I just keep doing one little thing, it's much easier to go back into the longer practice.

Don't quit until the miracle!

Dealing with Loss

Losing my husband was devastating. He was killed in an automobile accident. I just couldn't deal with it. I ran away. I did "a geographic." It was too painful.

Then finally, when I was able to get real, really feel what was happening, then I started to heal.

Loss is a part of everyone's life. I think it's to realize that loss is a normal part of being alive, and to accept it, and to know that it's just part of what goes on. We lose our childhoods as you get older. We lose people we love. The trees lose their leaves. It's just a process. It's about change. So I think, here again, it's about acceptance.

> Accept what is going on,
> and find something good to
> enjoy in the moment.

Forgiveness
Stopping Inappropriate Behavior

Forgiveness creates freedom and peace. When we forgive ourselves, we get a fresh chance to act differently while we are still alive. That's the important piece.

We've all done things that we're not happy about. We can look at "What can I do that will make it feel better?" If you see the person, you can tell them you're sorry. If the person has passed, you might want to write them a letter or do something nice for someone else.

But the biggest act of forgiveness is to stop inappropriate behavior. That's the biggest thing we can do. Change our behavior.

The forgiveness that comes from changing our behavior creates freedom.

Peace

Peace, for me, is a feeling that
there is no agitation going on
in my head or my body.

Peace comes from being real with God,
real with myself,
and real with other people.

Dove of Peace

The way you teach peace is to be peace.
It all begins with me. It all begins
with my meditation in the morning,
going to a peaceful place.

"Lord, take me where you want me to go.
Let me meet who you want me to meet.
Give me the words you want me to say.
And keep me out of your way."

~ Fr. Mychal Judge, American Franciscan

When you want
something good for somebody,
it's a prayer.

More About Mimi

Website
mimisammis.com

Instagram
Instagram.com/mimisammis

In 2018 Mimi has done a daily post inspired by *The Course in Miracles* on Instagram - paintings, photos & videos.

Facebook page
facebook.com/AnneMimiSammisLLC/

YouTube videos
www.youtube.com/user/mimisammis

- "Sculpting Peace a PBS Special about Mimi Sammis"
- "Love to Paint with Mimi Series" (multiple episodes)

Tsunami of Love
Breathing in a breath of love
and sending out a tsunami of love
to everyone around the globe!

Hosting the Tibetan Monks
I admire the work the monks do to
spread peace throughout the world.

Mimi is delighted to share her artistic process, philosophies of life, and her meditation practices. She encourages everyone to CREATE!

Lectures, Demonstrations, and Workshops

A group meets at her home weekly to share about their artistic endeavors. She also hosts a monthly artists salon.

"Share Night" is a highlight for many painters, poets, storytellers, writers, dancers, musicians, photographers, and a wide assortment of others who come to share their artistic creations or simply to watch and appreciate it all!

The Archbishop of Canterbury commissioned Mimi to create a sculpture in honor of the Golden Jubilee of Queen Elizabeth II. The piece is titled, "He Has the Whole World in His Hands."

"Mimi's most wonderful sculpture expresses so clearly the eternal love of God. The open hand, the tiny globe, and the dancing children depict the Father's care and the Father's heart."

The Arch Bishop of Canterbury, George L. Carey

Mimi has served on the United States National Committee for the Performing Arts. An honorary PhD, a Doctorate of Fine Arts, was awarded to Mimi by the University of Rhode Island in 2018.

One-Person Exhibitions

- United Nations, New York, New York
- The Hague, Netherlands
- American Embassy, Paris, France
- Temple Saint-Martial, Avignon, France
- American Embassy, Prague, Czech Republic
- National Sculpture Society, New York, New York
- Cathedral of St. John the Divine, New York, New York
- Wally Findlay Gallery, New York, New York
- US Olympics, Hilton Hotel, Lake Placid, New York
- Pepsi Company, Purchase, New York
- Jessica Hagen Fine Art & Design, Newport, Rhode Island
- International Tennis Hall of Fame, Newport, Rhode Island
- University of Rhode Island, Kingston, Rhode Island
- Madison State House, Madison, Wisconsin
- Vermont Arts Center, Inc., Manchester, Vermont
- Sally Harvey Gallery, Aspen, Colorado
- James Barker Gallery, Palm Beach, Florida
- The Bruce Museum, Greenwich, Connecticut

Public Sculpture Locations

- Lambeth Palace, London, England
- Unity School of Christianity, Unity Village, Michigan
- The Brockton Hospital, Brockton, Massachusetts
- Aspen Chapel, Aspen, Colorado
- Aspen Art Park, Rio Grande Trail, Colorado
- Greenwich Academy, Greenwich, Connecticut
- Westover School, Westover, Connecticut

In Rhode Island, USA

- T.F. Green Airport, Warwick
- The Children's Museum, Providence
- Narragansett Pier School, Narragansett
- Rhode Island Veterans Cemetery, Exeter
- Town of Narragansett, Narragansett
- Women and Infants Hospital, Providence

Works by Anne Mimi Sammis are also included in hundreds of private collections.

Dance of Peace

Narragansett Beach, Rhode Island, USA

Additional Books Published by All One World

all1world.com

CLEAR & FREE of Unwanted Thoughts & Emotions: 12 Effective Methods
Author: Ruth Shilling

Accessing Guidance: Intuitive Linked Communication (ILC)
Author: Frank DeMarco

Through A Medium's Eyes Series: About Life, Love, Mediumship, and the Spirit World
Rev. B. Anne Gehman, Volume 1
Carol Gasber, Volume 2
Neal Rzepkowski, M.D., Volume 3
Author: Ruth Shilling
mediumseyes.com

SUCCESS with the Violin & Life: Strategies, Techniques, and Tips for Learning Quickly and Doing Well
Author: Ruth Shilling
successviolin.com

Color It True Manifestation Mandalas: Adult Coloring Books that Draw Good Things to You! Volumes 1-4
A Short Explanation of Manifestation Principles with Art for Coloring by Ruth Shilling.

Made in the USA
Columbia, SC
21 January 2019